D1025333

Polar Animals

Polar Bears

by Emily Rose Townsend

Consulting Editor: Gail Saunders-Smith, Ph.D.
Consultant: Brock R. McMillan, Ph.D.
Associate Professor, Department of Biological Sciences
Minnesota State University, Mankato

Capstone
press

Mankato, Minnesota

Pebble Books are published by Capstone Press
151 Good Counsel Drive, P.O. Box 669, Mankato, Minnesota 56002
www.capstonepress.com

1 2 3 4 5 6 09 08 07 06 05 04

Library of Congress Cataloging-in-Publication Data
Townsend, Emily Rose.
    Polar bears / by Emily Rose Townsend.
    p. cm.—(Polar animals)
    Includes bibliographical references and index.
    Contents: Polar bears—Where polar bears live—Body parts—What polar
bears do.
    ISBN 0-7368-2358-1 (hardcover)
    1. Polar bear—Juvenile literature. [1. Polar bear. 2. Bears.] I.Title.
QL737.C27T68 2004
599.786—dc21   2003011401

Note to Parents and Teachers

The Polar Animals series supports national science standards
related to life science. This book describes and illustrates polar
bears. The photographs support early readers in understanding
the text. The repetition of words and phrases helps early readers
learn new words. This book also introduces early readers to
subject-specific vocabulary words, which are defined in the
Glossary. Early readers may need assistance to read some words
and to use the Table of Contents, Glossary, Read More, Internet
Sites, and Index/Word List sections of the book.

Table of Contents

Polar Bears 5

Where Polar Bears Live 9

Body Parts. 11

What Polar Bears Do 19

Glossary 22

Read More 23

Internet Sites 23

Index/Word List. 24

4

Polar Bears

Polar bears are large mammals with white fur.

Polar bears usually live alone.

land where polar bears live

icy areas where polar bears live

8

Where Polar Bears Live

Polar bears live along the coast in the Arctic. Polar bears also live on ice on the ocean.

Body Parts

Polar bears have long necks and big bodies.

Polar bears have fur to keep them warm. The white fur helps them blend with the ice and snow.

Polar bears have blubber to keep them warm.

Polar bears have large feet. Their feet help them walk on snow and ice. They also use their feet to swim.

What Polar Bears Do

Polar bears hunt
for seals that live
under ice in the Arctic.

Polar bears sleep
on snow and ice.

Glossary

Arctic—a cold region near the North Pole; polar bears live in the Arctic.

blubber—fat under the skin of some animals; blubber helps keep animals warm.

coast—land that is next to the ocean

fur—the soft, thick hairy coat of an animal

hunt—to find and kill animals for food

mammal—a warm-blooded animal that has a backbone; a mammal has hair or fur; female mammals feed milk to their young.

Read More

Kendell, Patricia. *Polar Bears.* In the Wild. Austin, Texas: Raintree Steck-Vaughn, 2003.

Murray, Julie. *Polar Bears.* Animal Kingdom. Edina, Minn.: Abdo, 2003.

Ring, Susan. *Polar Babies.* Step into Reading. New York: Random House, 2000.

Internet Sites

FactHound offers a safe, fun way to find Internet sites related to this book. All of the sites on FactHound have been researched by our staff.

Here's how:

1. Visit *www.facthound.com*
2. Type in this special code **0736823581** for age-appropriate sites. Or enter a search word related to this book for a more general search.
3. Click on the **Fetch It** button.

FactHound will fetch the best sites for you!

Index/Word List

alone, 7
Arctic, 9, 19
blend, 13
blubber, 15
bodies, 11
coast, 9
feet, 17
fur, 5, 13

hunt, 19
ice, 9, 13,
   17, 19, 21
large, 5, 17
live, 7, 9, 19
mammals, 5
necks, 11
ocean, 9

seals, 19
sleep, 21
snow, 13,
   17, 21
swim, 17
walk, 17
warm, 13, 15
white, 5, 13

Word Count: 106
Early-Intervention Level: 13

Editorial Credits
Mari C. Schuh, editor; Patrick D. Dentinger, designer; Scott Thoms, photo researcher;
   Karen Risch, product planning editor

Photo Credits
Bryan & Cherry Alexander/Seapics, 8
Cheryl A. Ertelt, 4
DigitalVision/Joel Simon, cover; Jeremy Woodhouse, 6
Joe McDonald, 1
Minden Pictures/Michio Hoshino, 10, 12, 16, 18
Steven Kazlowski/Seapics, 14
William Muñoz, 20